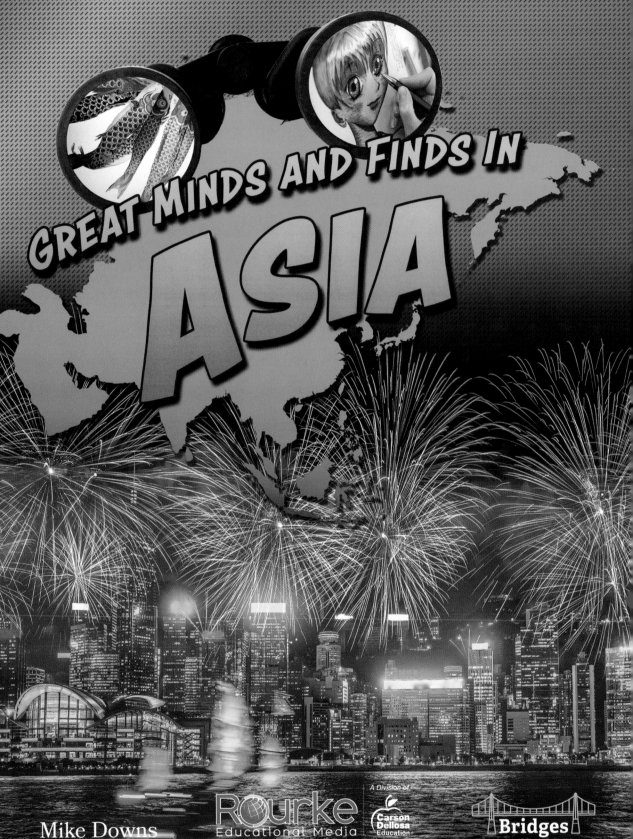

BEFORE AND DURING READING ACTIVITIES

Before Reading: *Building Background Knowledge and Vocabulary*

Building background knowledge can help children process new information and build upon what they already know. Before reading a book, it is important to tap into what children already know about the topic. This will help them develop their vocabulary and increase their reading comprehension.

Questions and Activities to Build Background Knowledge:

1. Look at the front cover of the book and read the title. What do you think this book will be about?

2. What do you already know about this topic?

3. Take a book walk and skim the pages. Look at the table of contents, photographs, captions, and bold words. Did these text features give you any information or predictions about what you will read in this book?

Vocabulary: *Vocabulary Is Key to Reading Comprehension*

Use the following directions to prompt a conversation about each word.

- Read the vocabulary words.
- What comes to mind when you see each word?
- What do you think each word means?

Vocabulary Words:

- alchemists
- binary
- cuneiform
- diverse
- gunpowder
- navigation
- nomadic
- sanitation
- terrain
- tundra

During Reading: *Reading for Meaning and Understanding*

To achieve deep comprehension of a book, children are encouraged to use close reading strategies. During reading, it is important to have children stop and make connections. These connections result in deeper analysis and understanding of a book.

Close Reading a Text

During reading, have children stop and talk about the following:

- Any confusing parts
- Any unknown words
- Text to text, text to self, text to world connections
- The main idea in each chapter or heading

Encourage children to use context clues to determine the meaning of any unknown words. These strategies will help children learn to analyze the text more thoroughly as they read.

When you are finished reading this book, turn to the next-to-last page for **Text-Dependent Questions** and an **Extension Activity**.

TABLE OF CONTENTS

WHERE IN THE WORLD IS ASIA?

Asia stretches from the southern island nation of Indonesia to the northern arctic **tundra** of Russia. Asia is the world's largest continent. About six of every ten people on Earth live there!

ASIA

Indonesian islands   *Russian tundra*

Asia has 49 countries, including India, China, Japan, Pakistan, and Turkey. Journey through Asia to discover its fascinating people and places. Find out about some of the ideas and inventions that come from this amazing part of the world.

Asia by the Numbers

Population: >4.5 billion

Size: >17 million square miles or >27 million square kilometers

Highest Point: Mount Everest, >29,035 feet or 8,850 meters

VOLCANOES, WATERFALLS, AND DRAGONS

Asia's land, animals, plants, and people are incredibly **diverse**. In Indonesia, you'll find active volcanoes and the world's largest lizard, the Komodo dragon. In Vietnam, you'll find magnificent waterfalls.

The waterfalls in Vietnam are visited by people from all over the world.

Nomadic Mongolians use eagles to hunt.

Mongolia is home to vast grasslands where **nomadic** communities live. China has the jagged Stone Forest and the brightly colored water plants of Red Beach. Mount Fuji in Japan attracts tourists as well as members of the Shinto religion to its shrines. Nepal has Mount Everest, where climbers reach the highest point on Earth.

Smelly Flower

A plant known as the corpse flower grows in the rainforests of Indonesia. It can weigh nearly 25 pounds (11.3 kilograms). It earned its nickname because it smells like rotting meat.

A WORLD OF WRITING

There is lots to discover in Asia about written words. An early form of writing was invented in Asia more than 5,000 years ago. It was invented in Mesopotamia, home to the ancient Sumerian civilization. Mesopotamia was located in what we now call Iraq, Kuwait, Syria, Turkey, and the surrounding areas.

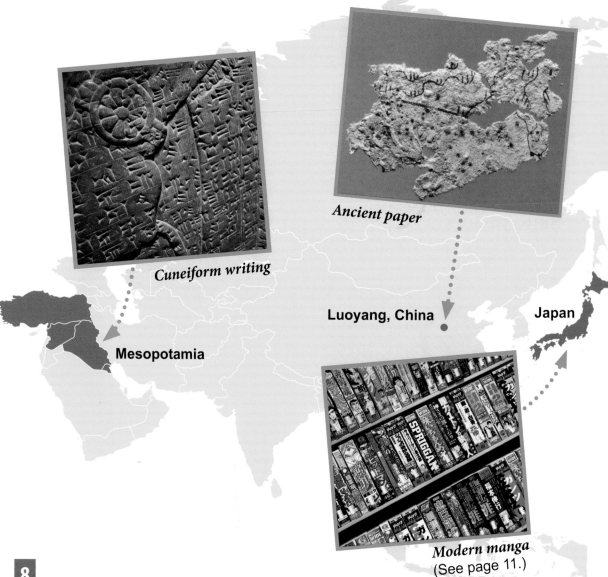

Cuneiform writing

Ancient paper

Mesopotamia

Luoyang, China

Japan

Modern manga
(See page 11.)

This new system was called **cuneiform**. It was written on clay tablets. The tablets were heavy and hard to move, so books were rare.

About 3,000 years later, early forms of paper were invented in Asia. Books made of paper were light enough to carry and sell. Reading and writing slowly spread throughout the world.

Artistic Writing

Each Chinese word is shown by a symbol rather than by a group of letters. There are tens of thousands of Chinese characters! These symbols can be written beautifully in calligraphy. This is a type of writing that is similar to painting. It is done using a brush and ink.

一　二　三　四　五
one　two　three　four　five

犬　貓　愛　喜　雲
dog　cat　love　happy　cloud

The first writer whose name is known for certain is the Mesopotamian priestess Enheduanna. She wrote religious poems and songs. Later, stories about an ancient Mesopotamian king were put together in the *Epic of Gilgamesh*. It is one of the oldest books.

The original Epic of Gilgamesh *was written on 12 clay tablets.*

The development of paper made it easier to record and share writing. The Chinese poet Li Qingzhao lived in the 12th century and wrote on paper. She became famous even though women were discouraged from writing at the time.

Li Qingzhao is one of China's greatest poets.

Many different written languages are used throughout Asia. People in some places use one of many alphabets. Others use systems of symbols.

Manga artist Osamu Tezuka is known as the "Father of manga." He made some of the most famous books in the world of manga.

Cool Comics

Manga are Japanese comics or graphic novels done in a modern style. *Manga* means "comics" in Japanese. The popularity of manga has spread throughout the world.

PROTECTING THE PEOPLE

Important Asian inventions include weapons and ways to protect people from attack. In about 221 BCE, the first emperor of China, Qin Shihuang, had to fight off fierce invaders from the north. To protect his territory, he ordered that walls stretching more than 3,000 miles (4,800 kilometers) be built. Other emperors added thousands of miles to the wall over the next 1,900 years.

The Great Wall is not a single wall but a group of different walls. It's no longer used to protect against invaders. The Great Wall is now a world-famous tourist attraction.

Common Era

We are living in the Common Era (CE). Ancient history happened before the Common Era (BCE).

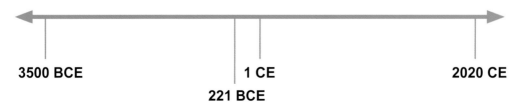

3500 BCE   1 CE   2020 CE

221 BCE

The Badaling section of the Great Wall has had more than 100,000 visitors in a single day.

Signal for Help

The Great Wall had signal towers built along its length. Many were built on top of ridges. Soldiers in the towers warned of attack by using smoke signals in daylight or fire at night.

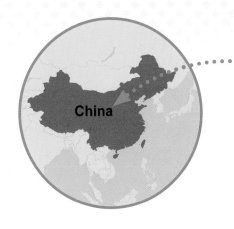

China

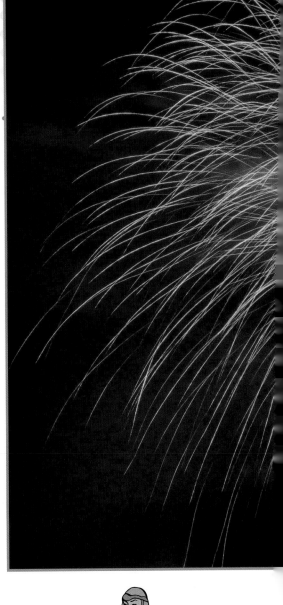

Ancient **alchemists** mixed chemicals hoping to discover the secret for long life. Instead, in about 850 CE, Chinese alchemists accidentally burned down their lab. They had discovered **gunpowder**.

The Chinese used their invention to make new weapons to fight off attackers. An early weapon was an arrow with a tube of gunpowder attached to it. Gunpowder would eventually be used in bullets, rockets, and many other weapons. It changed the way that wars were fought around the world.

The Chinese fire arrow was the earliest version of rockets and missiles used today.

Gunpowder is used in fireworks displays. Different chemicals are added to gunpowder to make different colors as the fireworks explode.

Noisy Celebrations

Before firecrackers were invented, Chinese people would heat up bamboo until it cracked and made a loud sound.
This is how we got the name "firecracker." The Chinese name for firecrackers, *baozhu*, means "exploding bamboo."

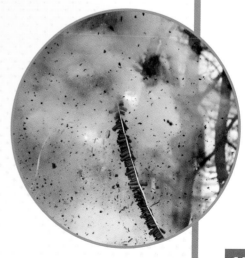

FLYING, FISHING, AND FUN

China

Indonesia

Kite festivals, such as this one in Bali, Indonesia, feature huge kites.

Kites are also an Asian invention. Some artists create paintings on kites. Others build impressive kites in shapes such as dragons or birds. Kites aren't just for entertainment, though. In Indonesia, kites are used to fish. A string with a hook is attached to the

Kites have provided entertainment for kids since ancient times.

kite. As the kite flies, the hook moves up and down in the water, attracting fish.

The earliest kites were invented in China and Indonesia. The Chinese military used them to measure distances across rough **terrain**. One emperor even made kites big enough to carry prisoners, who mostly crashed to the ground.

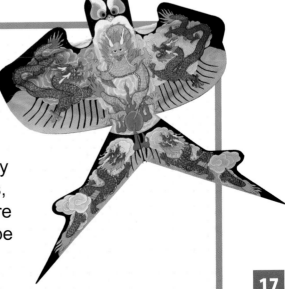

Colorful Sky

The Weifang kite festival in China includes kites of every variety. Dragons, octopuses, whales, pigs, and flowers are just a few shapes that can be found flying overhead.

USEFUL TECHNOLOGIES

Discoveries in Asia have led to technologies that improve people's lives. For example, computers are used all around us every day. They work using **binary** code.

Using zero as a number was first explained by the Indian mathematician Brahmagupta. Before this, there was not a number for the idea of "nothing." The use of the number zero soon led to advances in math and technology.

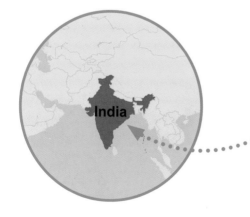

India

The Missile Woman

Tessy Thomas learned advanced math to become one of India's leading experts on ballistic missiles. She helped design a missile that could survive temperatures of 5,400 degrees Fahrenheit (3,000 degrees Celsius).

The Harappa sewage system is similar in some ways to what we use to keep cities clean in modern times.

Another discovery that improved everyday life was **sanitation**. People living in Harappa (in the area now called Pakistan) developed sanitation systems. These included ways to get water from wells. These systems also removed waste from homes. Systems like these are a vital part of cities and towns all over the world. Modern cities with millions of people, such as Tokyo, Japan, use advanced sanitation systems to keep people and homes clean. These systems sometimes involve technology that is popular in Asia, such as modern, high-tech toilets.

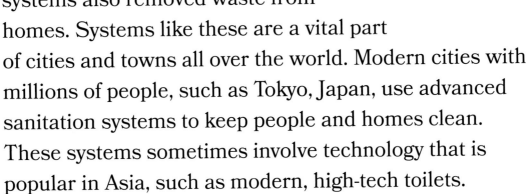

Harappa

Community members in Tokyo help sweep the streets to keep their city clean.

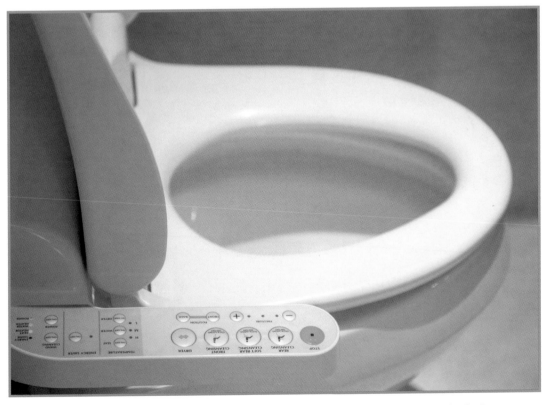

Some advanced toilets have automatic lid lifters, heated seats, and night lights.

Compasses are devices that can be used to find north, south, east, and west. They usually do this with Earth's natural magnetic forces. When they were first invented in China, they were used for something very different: arranging items to be in harmony with the environment. It wasn't until hundreds of years later that they were used for finding directions.

In early Chinese spoon compasses, the handle pointed south.

Qibla compass

Syria

Han Dynasty, China

Syrian astronomer Ibn al-Shatir built a device that combined a compass and a sundial. It could be used as a Qibla compass, which shows people in the Muslim religion which direction to face when praying. Magnetic compasses eventually became important instruments for **navigation**. Modern ships and planes use highly advanced compasses that can calculate and adjust for tiny movements.

Many ships still have compasses, but most people use information from satellites for navigation.

FOOD FOR THOUGHT

Delicious flavors and foods have been developed throughout Asia. There is Korean bulgogi, thin slices of grilled meat. Russia and nearby countries make traditional, delicious stuffed dumplings. You can thank Japanese chefs for making ramen, a type of thin noodle, popular around the world.

Other tasty treats are available too. Rice crackers and cakes, dried fish, and fruit jellies are popular among people of all ages. In some regions, crickets, palm weevils, and crunchy tarantulas are also common snacks.

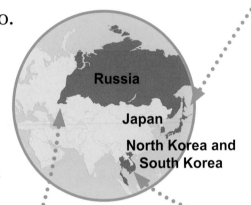

Russia

Japan

North Korea and South Korea

Dumplings

Popular toppings for ramen include egg, seaweed, and green onion.

Some bulgogi is cooked over a grill right at your table!

The Bug Chef

Chef Shoichi Uchiyama is world-famous for cooking with tasty bugs. He started cooking with them because they are highly nutritious and easy to grow. Would you eat some of Chef Uchiyama's dishes?

ROLLING ALONG

Can you imagine traveling over 300 miles (500 kilometers) per hour in a train? Japanese trains, called *Shinkansen* or bullet trains, can do it using high-tech wheels.

Wheels have been helping people move around Asia for a very long time. The Mesopotamians devised an easier way to move people and things around 3100 BCE when they attached wheels to their sleds. Wagons and wheeled toys soon followed. However, it wouldn't be until after 200 CE that a Chinese general invented

A single person can lift very heavy things with a wheelbarrow.

the wheelbarrow. It let people move heavy objects from one place to another. This allowed more trade. Horses and oxen could pull wagons filled with goods, moving a lot of supplies such as food at once along trade routes.

*Shinkansen **trains have changed travel for people all over Japan.***

An Important Road

One famous route was the Silk Road that connected Asia with Europe. It allowed countries in the Eastern and Western hemispheres to trade with each other regularly for the first time.

AMAZING ASIA

Asia is home to many amazing people and incredible discoveries. How would your life be different without the great minds and finds of Asia? The more you learn about this remarkable continent, the more amazing facts you'll uncover.

Russia

Syria

India

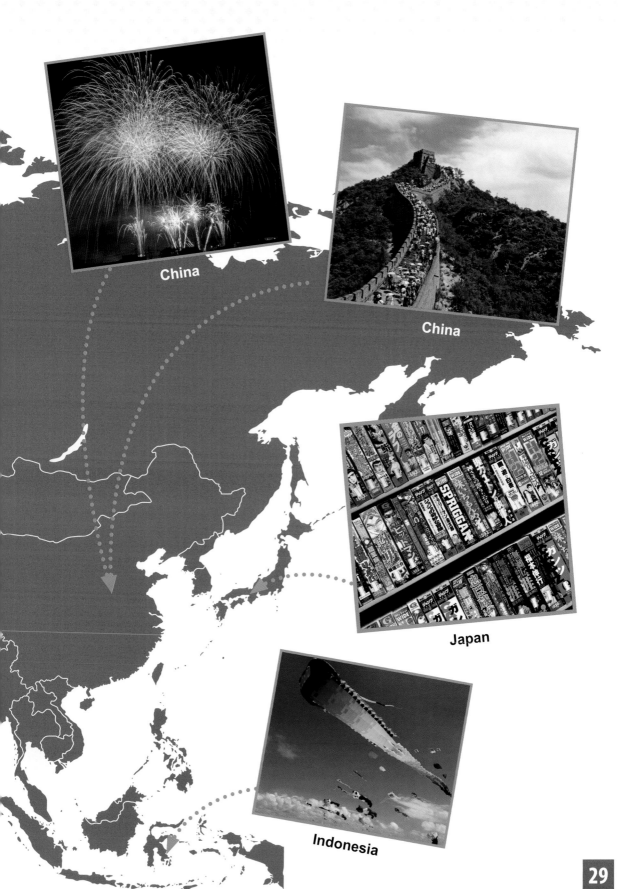

China

China

Japan

Indonesia

Glossary

alchemists (AL-kem-istz): ancient scientists that worked with chemicals

binary (BYE-ner-ee): made of 1s and 0s

cuneiform (kyoo-NEE-uh-form): an ancient writing system made of wedge shapes, usually used on clay tablets

diverse (dye-VURS): having many different types or kinds of something

gunpowder (GUHN-pou-dur): a powder that explodes easily

navigation (nav-i-GEY-shuhn): traveling in a specific direction to get from one place to another

nomadic (noh-MAD-ik): traveling from place to place instead of living in one area

sanitation (san-i-TAY-shuhn): methods of cleaning water and removing waste

terrain (tuh-RAYN): an area of land

tundra (TUHN-druh): a large area of ground that remains frozen and does not have trees

Index

Text-Dependent Questions

1. What were the alchemists searching for when they discovered gunpowder?

2. Why weren't there as many books before the invention of paper?

3. What do sanitation systems do?

4. How were compasses first used?

5. Why was the Great Wall of China built?

Extension Activity

Take a trip to Asia! Asia has thousands of interesting things to see. Where would you visit? Do some research about Asia. Choose a beach you would like to swim in, a mountain to climb, a river to paddle down, and a famous building or site you would like to see. List them in order of what you would like to do most.

About the Author

Mike Downs loves writing books about interesting places. He plans on visiting Asia soon. Mike already eats ramen and plans on trying some fried bugs when he has a chance.

www.rourkeeducationalmedia.com

PHOTO CREDITS: Cover: ©TK / TK; page 3: ©anurajrv / Pixabay; page 4: ©Puwadol Jaturawutthichai / Shutterstock.com; page 5: ©Marius Dobilas / Shutterstock.com (top left); page 5: ©Polarer / Shutterstock.com (top right); page 5: ©Arunna / iStockphoto.com (binoculars); page 6: ©Nguyen Quang Ngoc Tonkin / Shutterstock.com (top); page 6: ©GUDKOV ANDREY / Shutterstock.com (bottom); page 7: ©CW Pix / Shutterstock.com (top); page 7: ©Paul Marcus / Shutterstock.com (bottom); page 8: ©dikobraziy / Shutterstock.com (map); page 8: ©Aleksandr Stezhkin / Shutterstock.com (top left); page 8: ©Wikimedia (top right); page 8: ©Manakin / iStockphoto.com (bottom); page 9: ©chee gin tan / iStockphoto.com (top); page 9: ©colortone / Shutterstock.com; page 10: ©BabelStone / Wikimedia (top); page 10: ©Cui Cuo / Wikimedia (bottom); page 11: ©Piero Oliosi / Newscom (top); page 11: ©jemastock / iStockphoto.com (bottom); page 13: ©PEDRE / iStockphoto.com ; page 13: ©VOLLEX / Pixabay (fire); page 14: ©ArtMari / Shutterstock.com; page 15: ©DeltaWorks / Wikimedia (top); page 15: ©LP2 Studio / Shutterstock.com; page 16: ©Rido Zaen / Shutterstock.com; page 17: ©Pingun / Shutterstock.com (top); page 17: ©Dropu / Shutterstock.com; page 19: ©Valery Brozhinsky / Shutterstock.com (top); page 19: ©ZargonDesign / iStockphoto.com (missile); page 19: ©Hindustan Times / Newscom (bottom); page 20: ©Iftekkhar / Shutterstock.com; page 21: ©Kekyalyaynen / Shutterstock.com (top); page 21: ©Ratchat / iStockphoto.com (bottom); page 22: ©Maqivi / Wikimedia (left); page 22: © / Wikimedia (right); page 23: ©ewg3D / iStockphoto.com ; page 24: ©Tatiana Bralnina / Shutterstock.com; page 25: ©PamelaJoeMcFarlane / iStockphoto.com (top); page 25: ©gkrphoto / Shutterstock.com (middle); page 25: ©Splash News / Newscom (bottom); page 24: ©Marzolino / Shutterstock.com; page 25: ©Blanscape / Shutterstock.com (top); page 25: ©Maxiphoto / iStockphoto.com (bottom); background: ©DavidZydd / Pixabay

Edited by: Tracie Santos
Cover layout by: Kathy Walsh
Interior layout by: Book Buddy Media

Library of Congress PCN Data

Great Minds and Finds in Asia / Mike Downs
(Discoveries Around the World)
ISBN 978-1-73163-794-9 (hard cover)(alk. paper)
ISBN 978-1-73163-871-7 (soft cover)
ISBN 978-1-73163-948-6 (e-Book)
ISBN 978-1-73164-025-3 (ePub)
Library of Congress Control Number: 2020930256

Rourke Educational Media
Printed in the United States of America
01-1662011937